EYEWITNESS TO HISTORY

THOMAS JEFFERSON

in his own words

Gareth Stevens
Publishing

By John Shea

Please visit our website, www.garethstevens.com. For a free color catalog of all our high-quality books, call toll free 1-800-542-2595 or fax 1-877-542-2596.

Library of Congress Cataloging-in-Publication Data

Shea, John M.
Thomas Jefferson in his own words / by John M. Shea.
 p. cm. — (Eyewitnesses to history)
Includes index.
ISBN 978-1-4339-9933-8 (pbk.)
ISBN 978-1-4824-3317-3 (6-pack)
ISBN 978-1-4339-9873-7 (library binding)
1. Jefferson, Thomas, — 1743-1826 — Juvenile literature. 2. Presidents — United States — Biography — Juvenile literature. I. Shea, John M. II. Title.
E332.79 S54 2014
973.4—dc23

First Edition

Published in 2014 by
Gareth Stevens Publishing
111 East 14th Street, Suite 349
New York, NY 10003

Copyright © 2014 Gareth Stevens Publishing

Designer: Katelyn E. Reynolds
Editor: Therese Shea

Photo credits: Cover, p. 1 (Jefferson) Hulton Archive/Getty Images; cover, p. 1 (background illustration) MPI/Getty Images; cover, p. 1 (logo quill icon) Seamartini Graphics Media/Shutterstock.com; cover, p. 1 (logo stamp) YasnaTen/Shutterstock.com; cover, p. 1 (color grunge frame) DmitryPrudnichenko/Shutterstock.com; cover, pp. 1-32 (paper background) Nella/Shutterstock.com; cover, pp. 1-32 (decorative elements) Ozerina Anna/Shutterstock.com; pp. 1-32 (wood texture) Reinhold Leitner/Shutterstock.com; pp. 1-32 (open book background) Elena Schweitzer/Shutterstock.com; pp. 1-32 (bookmark) Robert Adrian Hillman/Shutterstock.com; pp. 5, 8-9, 21 Hulton Archive/Getty Images; p. 7 MPI/Getty Images; p. 11 Photos.com/Thinkstock.com; pp. 12-13 Culture Club/Getty Images; p. 15 Universal History Archive/Getty Images; p. 17 Popperfoto/Getty Images; pp. 18-19 DeAgostini/Getty Images; pp. 22-23 Stock Montage/Getty Images; p. 25 FPG/Archive Photos/Getty Images; p. 27 (signature) McSush/Wikipedia.com; p. 27 (illustration) Three Lions/Getty Images.

Printed in the United States of America

CPSIA compliance information: Batch #CW14GS: For further information contact Gareth Stevens, New York, New York at 1-800-542-2595.

CONTENTS

*Words in the glossary appear in **bold** type the first time they are used in the text.*

A FATHER
of a Nation

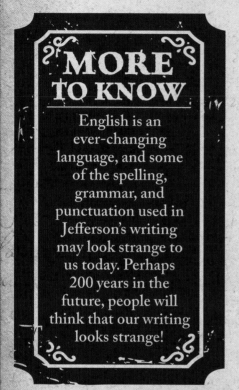
There are few people as significant and as fascinating in American history as Thomas Jefferson. He was a president of the United States, the founder of the University of Virginia, and the primary writer of the Declaration of Independence, a **document** that shaped both US and world history. He was a member of the Second Continental Congress when it voted for independence from the British, and he was the first US secretary of state under George Washington, the nation's first president.

Jefferson was an enthusiastic writer—he wrote around 28,000 letters in his lifetime! Though he lived more than 175 years ago, Jefferson's writings give us a deeper understanding of this man and the important events he witnessed.

Thomas Jefferson served his nation for over five decades. Because of his talents as a writer and his presence at so many historic events, Thomas Jefferson was an important eyewitness to the birth of the United States.

READING AND WRITING

By many accounts, Thomas Jefferson wasn't a gifted public speaker, but he was recognized as a very talented writer. Perhaps some of that talent was due to his love of reading. He once remarked to his friend (and sometimes political rival) John Adams, *"I cannot live without books."*

To John's wife, Abigail Adams, Jefferson confessed that his *"greatest of all amusements, [is] reading."*

EARLY *Life*

JULIAN AND GREGORIAN CALENDARS

In 1582, Pope Gregory XIII recognized that the old Julian calendar (named after Julius Caesar) was flawed. Therefore, he approved a new calendar removing 11 days. England and its colonies adopted the Gregorian calendar in 1752, and it's still in use today. So while sometimes Jefferson is said to have been born April 2, 1743 (according to the Julian calendar), he was born April 13, 1743, according to the Gregorian calendar.

Thomas Jefferson was born on April 13, 1743, near Charlottesville, Virginia. Jefferson described his father, Peter, as having *"a strong mind, sound judgment and [being] eager after information, he read much and improved himself."* These were qualities that Jefferson shared with his father. Thomas Jefferson began school when he was 5 years old. He was studying Latin, Greek, and French by the age of 9.

In 1760, Jefferson attended the College of William and Mary, where he studied 15 hours a day and practiced the violin for several more hours! Even at this early age, Jefferson believed strongly in the importance of education. *"Knowledge indeed is a desirable, a lovely possession,"* he later wrote to his son-in-law Thomas Mann Randolph. After college, Jefferson studied law and became a lawyer in 1767.

Established in 1693, the College of William and Mary is the second-oldest college in the United States (after Harvard University).
Four American presidents graduated from there: George Washington, Thomas Jefferson, James Monroe, and John Tyler.

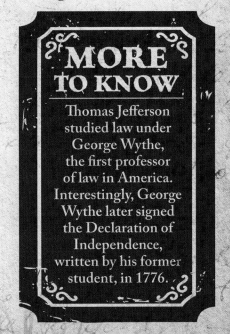

MORE TO KNOW

Thomas Jefferson studied law under George Wythe, the first professor of law in America. Interestingly, George Wythe later signed the Declaration of Independence, written by his former student, in 1776.

JEFFERSON

Begins His Political Life

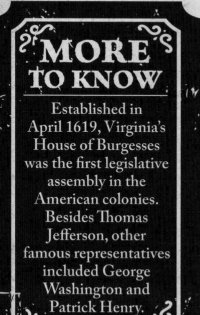
In 1769, Thomas Jefferson began serving in colonial Virginia's legislature, the House of Burgesses. *"I made one effort in that body for the permission of the* **emancipation** *of slaves, which was rejected,"* Jefferson wrote in his **autobiography**. Ending slavery in America seemed to be a passion for Jefferson at times. He said slavery was a *"cruel war against human nature itself, violating its most sacred rights of life & liberties."*

Monticello served as Jefferson's home until his death in 1826. It covered about 5,000 acres (2,025 ha).

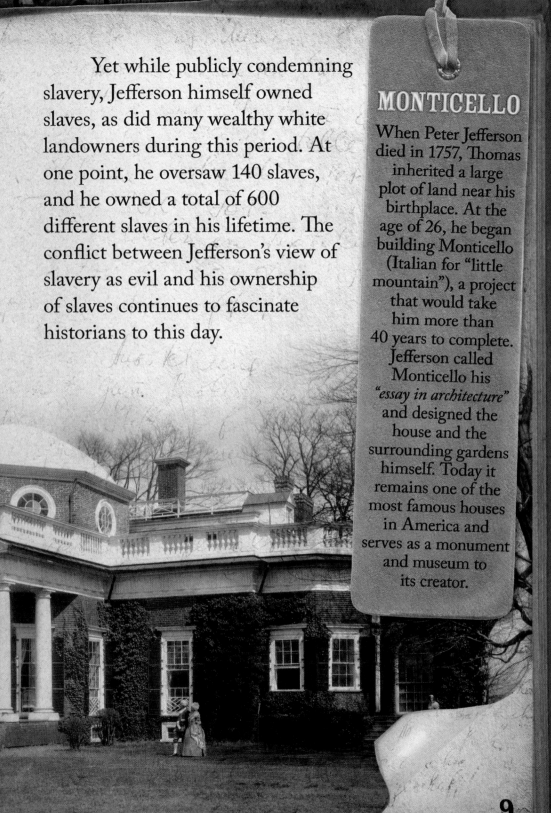

Yet while publicly condemning slavery, Jefferson himself owned slaves, as did many wealthy white landowners during this period. At one point, he oversaw 140 slaves, and he owned a total of 600 different slaves in his lifetime. The conflict between Jefferson's view of slavery as evil and his ownership of slaves continues to fascinate historians to this day.

MONTICELLO

When Peter Jefferson died in 1757, Thomas inherited a large plot of land near his birthplace. At the age of 26, he began building Monticello (Italian for "little mountain"), a project that would take him more than 40 years to complete. Jefferson called Monticello his *"essay in architecture"* and designed the house and the surrounding gardens himself. Today it remains one of the most famous houses in America and serves as a monument and museum to its creator.

RISING
Tensions

In the 1760s and 1770s, British **Parliament** placed taxes on items such as sugar, paper, and tea, which made the American colonists angry. Relations between England and its colonies worsened. In 1774, Parliament passed laws called the Coercive Acts to strengthen its hold on Massachusetts and punish the colonists for the Boston Tea Party and other rebellious acts.

But by punishing Massachusetts, England caused the colonies to unify. It had become important to come to *"an understanding with all the other colonies,"* Jefferson observed, and *"to produce an unity of action."* The First Continental Congress met September 1774 in Philadelphia, Pennsylvania. Too ill to attend, Jefferson sent on a document he wrote called

In 1765, Jefferson witnessed Patrick Henry propose the Virginia Stamp Act Resolutions, which argued that only the people, or representatives elected by the people, could impose taxes. Henry argued that since Virginians had no elected representatives in British Parliament, only the House of Burgesses had the power to tax the people of Virginia. Henry's ideas were very extreme at this time, but Jefferson was impressed with the *"splendid display of Mr. Henry's talents as a popular **orator**."*

"A Summary View of the Rights of British America." In it, he argued that British Parliament had no authority over the colonies.

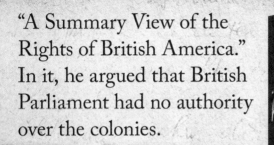

The Tea Act of 1773 required American colonists to buy tea from only one company. In protest, Bostonians who had dressed as Native Americans boarded trade ships and dumped 342 crates of tea into Boston Harbor.

A DECLARATION
of Independence

In April 1775, tensions between England and the colonies erupted into gunfire. British soldiers marched on Lexington and Concord in Massachusetts to seize colonists' arms. Colonial forces met them, resulting in nearly 100 dead or wounded colonists. News of the bloodshed angered many Americans. A *"frenzy of revenge seems to have seized all ranks of people,"* Jefferson observed. The American Revolution had begun.

MORE TO KNOW

Even while asking for peace, Congress was also working on a new government. Thomas Jefferson contributed to the early drafts of the Articles of Confederation and Perpetual Union, the framework for a new government after American independence.

Before 1770, there had been no formal organization uniting the colonies. Because of the crisis with England, the Continental Congresses became America's first national governments.

In May 1775, the Second Continental Congress met and, this time, Thomas Jefferson attended. Congress prepared for war. They appointed George Washington as commander in chief of the colonists' army, the Continental army. Congress asked Jefferson to write a statement explaining why the colonies were going to war. In "A Declaration of the Causes & Necessity for Taking Up Arms," Jefferson explained: *"Our attachment to no nation on earth should **supplant** our attachment to liberty."*

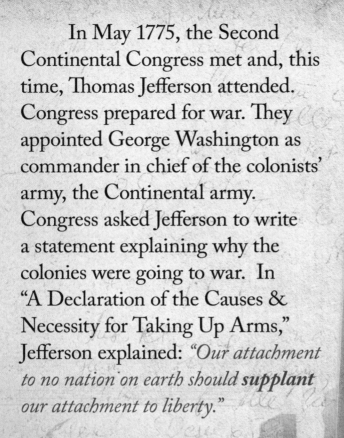

THE OLIVE BRANCH PETITION

Many people, including members of the Second Continental Congress, were still hoping for peace. In June 1775, Congress sent the Olive Branch **Petition**, which stated the colonists' loyalty to King George III and asked him for a peaceful end to the fighting. King George III refused to read the petition, but instead sent more soldiers to the colonies. This angered many colonists and further strengthened the case for independence.

Of the many words Jefferson said and wrote over his lifetime, perhaps none have inspired more people than those in the Declaration of Independence: *"all men are created equal."* Both Abraham Lincoln and Martin Luther King Jr. quoted Jefferson in speeches supporting freedom and rights for African Americans. In 1848, Elizabeth Cady Stanton argued for women's rights in her "Declaration of Sentiments" by adapting Jefferson's words: *"all men and women are created equal."*

Even while preparing for war, many colonists didn't want to break away from England. Jefferson noted that the *"idea that we had friends in England worth keeping . . . still haunted the minds of many."* Still, as the war continued, more people saw independence as the best course of action.

On June 7, 1776, Richard Henry Lee of Virginia proposed that the Second Continental Congress declare the colonies to be free from England. John Adams agreed with Lee and persuaded the other delegates *"with a power of thought and expression that moved us from our seats,"* Jefferson observed.

Jefferson was asked to write a statement declaring the independence of the American colonies to the world. The resulting document, the Declaration of Independence, is considered one of the most important documents in the history of **democracy**.

The Declaration of Independence was adopted by the Second Continental Congress on July 4, 1776, but it wasn't signed by the delegates until August 2. One member, Thomas McKean, didn't sign it until 1781.

While Jefferson (right) wrote most of the Declaration of Independence in 3 weeks during the summer of 1776, John Adams (middle) and Benjamin Franklin (left) helped by making suggestions.

A RETURN
to Virginia

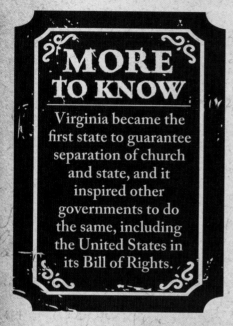

MORE TO KNOW

Virginia became the first state to guarantee separation of church and state, and it inspired other governments to do the same, including the United States in its Bill of Rights.

In the fall of 1776, Thomas Jefferson retired from the Second Continental Congress. He wanted to help Virginia form its new state government. *"I thought I could be of more use in forwarding that work,"* Jefferson later wrote in his autobiography. He was elected to the House of Delegates, which replaced the House of Burgesses.

Jefferson believed government shouldn't involve itself in matters of its citizens' beliefs if those beliefs don't harm others. He wrote, *"The legitimate powers of government extend to such acts only as are injurious to others. But it does me no injury for my neighbour to say there are twenty gods, or no god."* Jefferson considered the Virginia **Statute** for Religious Freedom, which became law in 1786, one of his most important writings.

Jefferson had many interests besides politics. He wrote about science, architecture, agriculture, education, geography, and music.

JAMES MADISON

When Jefferson first proposed the Virginia Statute for Religious Freedom in the late 1770s, many in the House of Delegates opposed it and prevented it from passing into law. One delegate who did support it, however, was James Madison. Madison and Jefferson shared many interests and beliefs, and they became good friends over the years. It was Madison who finally pushed the statute to become a law in 1786 while Jefferson was living in France.

In June 1779, Thomas Jefferson was elected governor of Virginia. The British were attacking the southern states, including Virginia, and Jefferson himself was almost captured by the British army. He decided not to run for reelection in 1781. He thought the people of Virginia *"would have more confidence in a Military chief"* to lead them during the war.

Jefferson retired from public life and returned to Monticello to spend time with his family and to write. In September 1782, Jefferson's wife Martha died, and he fell into a deep depression. In November 1782, George Washington asked Jefferson to help with peace talks with England. Jefferson agreed. However, before he could set sail, news arrived in America that John Adams, Benjamin Franklin, and John Jay reached a peace agreement with England.

MARTHA JEFFERSON

Martha Wayles Skelton married Thomas Jefferson on January 1, 1772. There are no portraits of Martha, but her granddaughter Ellen Randolph Coolidge described her as *"a very attractive person"* and *"a graceful, ladylike and accomplished woman."* She and Thomas were very happy together. She was *"the cherished companion of my life,"* he wrote after her death. *"I had lived the last ten years in . . . happiness."* Like her husband, Martha is buried at Monticello.

MORE TO KNOW

Thomas Jefferson was originally asked to join John Adams, Benjamin Franklin, and John Jay in peace talks with England in 1781. However, Jefferson declined because he didn't want to be away from his family.

For more than 8 years, George Washington led a poorly trained and equipped Continental army against the larger and more powerful British army. Washington defeated British general Charles Cornwallis at Yorktown, Virginia, in October 1781 at the last major battle of the American Revolution.

ARTICLES OF
Confederation

During the war, the states had begun a "league of friendship" under the first **constitution**, the Articles of Confederation. British king George III had made Americans suspicious of a strong central ruling power, so the Articles limited the power of the national government. However, it soon became clear that the Articles weren't enough to govern this new nation.

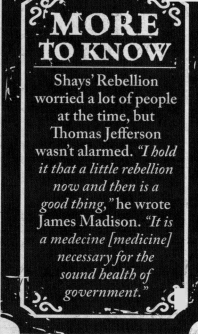

MORE TO KNOW

Shays' Rebellion worried a lot of people at the time, but Thomas Jefferson wasn't alarmed. *"I hold it that a little rebellion now and then is a good thing,"* he wrote James Madison. *"It is a medecine [medicine] necessary for the sound health of government."*

Many American farmers who fought in the American Revolution found themselves with great debt after the war. Some were put in prison, and others had their farms taken away. In 1786, Daniel Shays of Massachusetts led a large group of armed farmers to the state courthouse to protest the way they were being treated. Among other issues, Shays' Rebellion made many Americans realize they needed a stronger government if they were going to survive as a new nation.

Daniel Shays had been a well-respected military leader who rose to the rank of captain during the American Revolution. A farmer is shown here attacking a government official during Shays' Rebellion.

JEFFERSON IN FRANCE

From 1784 to 1789, Jefferson was a diplomat in France. He helped his good friend Marquis de Lafayette write a document which would become France's "Declaration of the Rights of Man." Jefferson was initially a strong supporter of the French Revolution because he thought the citizens' rebellion against French king Louis XVI was similar to the colonies' rebellion against England's George III. However, his support dimmed when the violence and bloodshed in France continued to grow.

THE FEDERAL
Constitution

To raise money, the federal government placed a tax on whiskey. This tax was very unpopular among many farmers. Jefferson thought the government made a mistake: *"the first error was to pass it [the whiskey tax]; the second was to enforce it."* In 1794, when farmers attacked tax collectors, the federal government sent soldiers in to stop the rebellion. It was considered a successful demonstration of power for the new government.

The Constitutional **Convention** met in Philadelphia between May and September of 1787 to discuss how to strengthen the national government. Jefferson was in France, but James Madison sent him a draft of the new Constitution.

In general, Jefferson liked the Constitution but thought it needed to guarantee the freedoms and rights of US citizens. There needed to be a *"bill of rights,"* Jefferson wrote to Madison, *"providing . . . freedom of religion, freedom of the press . . . and trials by jury."* Many agreed with Jefferson, and the states approved the new Constitution with an understanding that such guarantees would be added. In 1789, the first Congress of the new central, or federal, government proposed 12 amendments to the Constitution. Ten were accepted and became known as the Bill of Rights.

The State House in Philadelphia was the site of both the approval of the Declaration of Independence and the Constitutional Convention. It's now appropriately called Independence Hall.

MORE TO KNOW

The original purpose of the Constitutional Convention was to change the Articles of Confederation, not to write a brand-new constitution. Jefferson described the convention as *"an assembly of **demigods**,"* a mix of the intelligent and resourceful men who had created a nation.

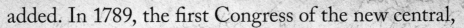

THE RISE OF
American Political Parties

In 1790, Jefferson became the first secretary of state under President George Washington. However, he disagreed with other members of Washington's staff about the power of the federal government.

Alexander Hamilton, John Adams, and some others believed the Constitution allowed the federal government powers beyond the ones clearly stated. They were called Federalists. But Jefferson argued, *"To take a single step beyond the boundaries . . . is to take possession of a boundless field of power."* Such power was very close to having a king, Jefferson believed. He thought the Federalists had a *"preference of kingly over **republican** government."* In 1793, Jefferson resigned.

MORE TO KNOW

Jefferson and James Madison formed the first American political party: the Democratic-Republicans. They were united, as Jefferson wrote, *"in the same principles and pursuits of what [we] deemed for the greatest good of our country."*

In 1796, Jefferson ran for president as a Democratic-Republican against Federalist John Adams. Jefferson lost the election by three votes, which made him vice president under Adams.

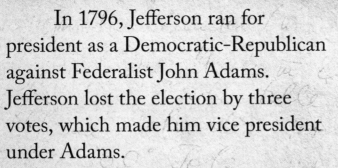

Alexander Hamilton (second from right) was the first secretary of treasury. He believed the US Constitution gave the government power to create a national bank, a view with which Jefferson strongly disagreed.

THE TWELFTH AMENDMENT

Under the Constitution, the person receiving the most votes became president, while the person receiving the second-most votes became vice president. This proved disastrous with Adams and Jefferson, two men with very different political ideas. Indeed, they rarely talked to each other during the 4 years of Adams's presidency. The Twelfth Amendment, passed in 1804, allowed for separate votes for president and for vice president to help prevent members of different parties from serving together.

In 1800, Jefferson and Adams once again ran for president, and this time Jefferson won. This was the first peaceful transfer of power from one political party to another in the United States' young history. The *"revolution of 1800 . . . was as real a revolution in the principles of our government as that of [17]76,"* Jefferson later recalled.

During his two terms, Jefferson cut the national debt while reducing taxes, including the unpopular Whiskey Tax. Perhaps his most notable act was the purchase of the Louisiana Territory in 1803. Although some wondered if, under the Constitution, Jefferson had the authority to buy such a large piece of land from France, Jefferson believed it was for the good of the country. He asked, *"Is it not better that the . . . [land] be settled by our own brethren and children, than by strangers of another family?"*

LEWIS AND CLARK EXPEDITION

In 1803, most Americans lived within 50 miles (80 km) of the Atlantic Ocean. Jefferson sent Meriwether Lewis, William Clark, and more than 40 men across the Northwest to the Pacific Ocean in 1804 to map routes, establish trade with Native Americans, and collect information about unexplored land. Jefferson was interested in encouraging movement west. *"Those who come after us will fill up the canvas we begin,"* predicted Jefferson.

Jefferson's actual signature:

Th: Jefferson

The US Senate voted to allow Jefferson to purchase the Louisiana Territory to expand the United States.

The UNIVERSITY
of Virginia

MORE TO KNOW

Later in life, Jefferson resumed his friendship with John Adams. Incredibly, both men died hours apart and exactly 50 years after the adoption of the Declaration of Independence.

After his presidency, Jefferson retired from political office, but he didn't stop his public service. He turned to his passion for education, this time for others. *"Above all things I hope the education of the common people will be attended to,"* Jefferson wrote to James Madison. With Jefferson and Madison in attendance, the first cornerstone of what would become the University of Virginia was placed in 1817.

Establishing the University of Virginia was one of Jefferson's proudest accomplishments: *"It is the last act of usefulness I can **render**, and could I see it open I would not ask an hour more of life."* The university opened in 1825, and Jefferson lived to see that day. He died the next year on July 4, 1826, at the age of 83.

TIMELINE
THE LIFE OF THOMAS JEFFERSON

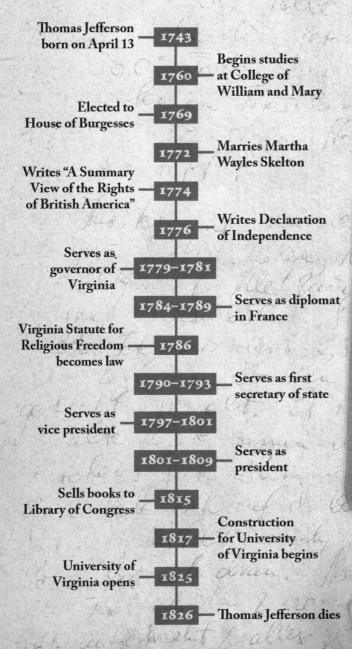

1743	Thomas Jefferson born on April 13
1760	Begins studies at College of William and Mary
1769	Elected to House of Burgesses
1772	Marries Martha Wayles Skelton
1774	Writes "A Summary View of the Rights of British America"
1776	Writes Declaration of Independence
1779–1781	Serves as governor of Virginia
1784–1789	Serves as diplomat in France
1786	Virginia Statute for Religious Freedom becomes law
1790–1793	Serves as first secretary of state
1797–1801	Serves as vice president
1801–1809	Serves as president
1815	Sells books to Library of Congress
1817	Construction for University of Virginia begins
1825	University of Virginia opens
1826	Thomas Jefferson dies

LIBRARY OF CONGRESS

The Library of Congress was started in 1800 by President John Adams, but the original collection was burned by the British during the War of 1812. Jefferson had spent over 50 years collecting books, and he offered his 6,487 books as a replacement. Jefferson described his collection as containing *"everything which related to America, and indeed whatever was rare and valuable in every science."* Today, the Library of Congress contains more than 35 million books.

29

GLOSSARY

autobiography: a book written by someone about their own life

constitution: the basic laws by which a country or state is governed

convention: a gathering of people who have a common interest or purpose

demigod: a person so outstanding that they seem almost like a god

democracy: a government in which every person has a free and equal right to participate

document: a formal piece of writing

emancipation: the act of freeing from the restraint, control, or power of another, usually referring to the freeing of slaves

orator: one who gives speeches, especially in a formal setting

Parliament: the lawmaking body of England, now the United Kingdom

petition: a written request signed by many people demanding an action from an authority or government

render: to give help or provide a service

republican: having to do with a form of government in which people elect representatives to make laws

statute: a law

supplant: to take the place of something

FOR MORE
Information

Books

Anderson, Michael, ed. *Thomas Jefferson*. New York, NY:
Britannica Educational Publishing, 2013.

Chew, Elizabeth. *Thomas Jefferson: A Day at Monticello*. New
York, NY: Abrams Books For Young Readers, 2013.

Domnauer, Teresa. *The Lewis & Clark Expedition*. New York,
NY: Children's Press, 2013.

Websites

The Declaration of Independence
www.ushistory.org/declaration/
Run by the Independence Hall Association of Philadelphia,
this website contains a lot of interesting facts about the
Declaration of Independence and the American Revolution.

Thomas Jefferson's Monticello
www.monticello.org
This website contains information about Thomas Jefferson's
famous home and about Jefferson himself, including
his writings.

INDEX